KALEIDOSCOPE OF CREATURES

WRITTEN BY CATH ARD

ILLUSTRATED BY GREER STOTHERS

WIDE EYED EDITIONS

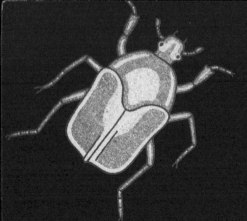

CONTENTS

WELCOME TO THE WORLD OF COLOR

The world is a kaleidoscope of creatures!
This book will take you on a rainbow safari, where
you will meet the most colorful creatures from the
skies, woods, jungles, and seas.

Over eight million different animals swoop, swim,
stalk, and slither across our planet, and they come in
every imaginable shade and pattern under the sun.
But what is the reason behind their beautiful colors?

From rainbow-feathered birds and cats with fancy fur to
fish with glittering scales and frogs with deadly skin—these
incredible coverings all have a job to do. Color and pattern
help animals to survive and thrive.

While some animals blend into their background, others
prefer the art of disguise, imitating another animal or object
to stay safe or to trick prey. Bold patterns and glowing
colors can help creatures to charm a mate—or to flash
a warning to enemies.

Many animals go for a full coat of color, while others have just one eye-catching splash. Different coverings can be good for warming up or cooling down, gripping or sliding, protecting or defending.

There are creatures that change their appearance as they grow and others that can switch their look in the blink of an eye.

Sometimes coverings can help us tell males from females, young from old, weak from strong.

Whatever their purpose, creature colors and patterns make our world a more interesting and beautiful place. So, let's celebrate every shade, speckle, and fleck of this wild kaleidoscope, from the tiniest, shimmering wings to the biggest, stripy skins!

ANIMAL FAMILY TREE

We share the planet with millions of different living things, from tiny bugs to mega beasts. Scientists make sense of them all by sorting animals into groups. An elephant and a mouse look different, but they have things in common that mean they are both mammals.

MAMMALS
- Usually have hair or fur
- Give birth to live young
- Breathe with lungs
- Feed young with their milk

BIRDS
- Covered in feathers
- Have wings, beaks, and scaly legs
- Breathe with lungs
- Young hatch from hard-shelled eggs

REPTILES
- Have dry, scaly skin
- Most lay eggs
- Fully formed young hatch out
- Breathe with lungs

AMPHIBIANS
- Live in damp places
- Breathe with lungs and through their skin
- Young hatch from eggs

FISH
- Live in water
- Breathe through slits called gills
- Have scaly skin
- Have fins and tails for swimming

WARM-BLOODED
These animals can control their body temperature

COLD-BLOODED
These animals need the sun's heat to warm their bodies

VERTEBRATES
Animals that have a backbone

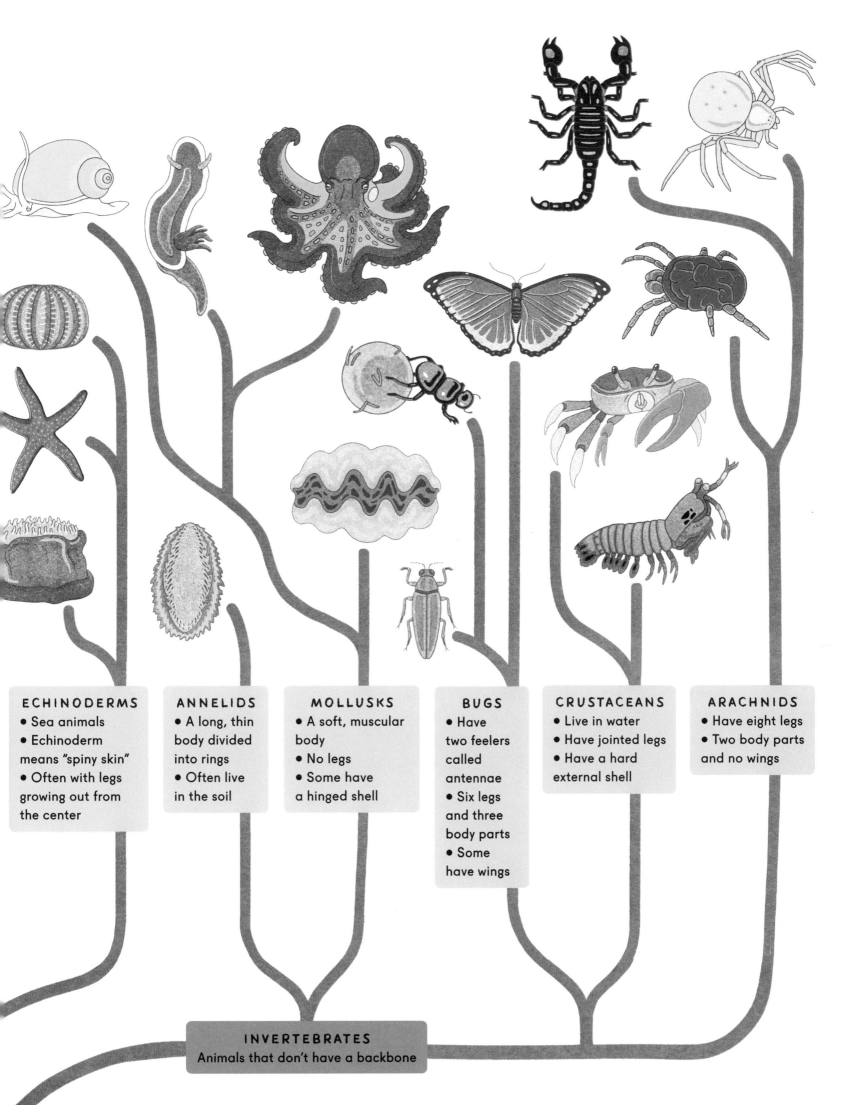

ECHINODERMS
- Sea animals
- Echinoderm means "spiny skin"
- Often with legs growing out from the center

ANNELIDS
- A long, thin body divided into rings
- Often live in the soil

MOLLUSKS
- A soft, muscular body
- No legs
- Some have a hinged shell

BUGS
- Have two feelers called antennae
- Six legs and three body parts
- Some have wings

CRUSTACEANS
- Live in water
- Have jointed legs
- Have a hard external shell

ARACHNIDS
- Have eight legs
- Two body parts and no wings

INVERTEBRATES
Animals that don't have a backbone

FEATHERS, FUR, SCALES AND SKIN

DAMP SKIN

Amphibians breathe through their thin, moist skin. These animals need to stay damp to survive.
- Some have smooth skin, others have lumpy skin.
- Brightly colored skin acts as a warning to predators.
- Deadly poison oozes from the skin of some amphibians.

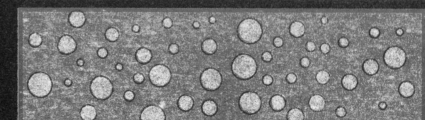

FUR

All mammals have some fur or hair on their bodies for warmth. But fur can do more than just keep a mammal warm.
- Patterned and colored fur can provide camouflage.
- Oil in fur helps to keep animals dry.
- Strong, sharp hairs help some animals to defend themselves.

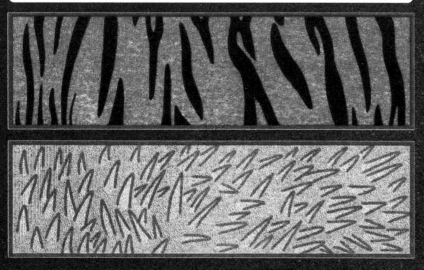

REPTILE SCALES

Most reptiles have scales. All scales are waterproof, so swimmers don't get soaked and desert reptiles don't dry out.
- Colored scales help animals to blend in.
- Thick, prickly scales act like a coat of armor.
- Smooth scales slide and rough scales grip.

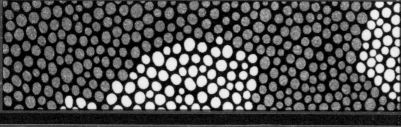

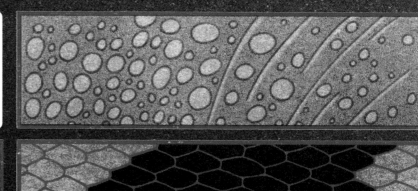

8

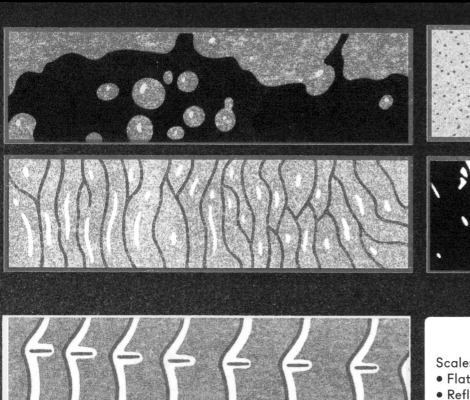

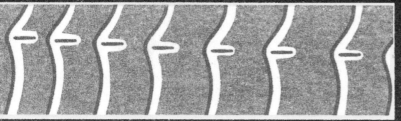

FISH SCALES

Scales give fish protection from predators and infections.
- Flat, overlapping scales help fish swim fast through the water.
- Reflective scales flash and dazzle predators.
- Colored scales send out a warning or help fish to blend in.

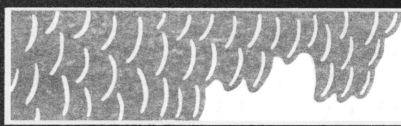

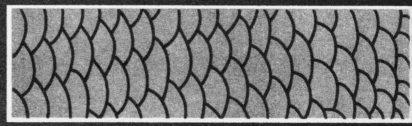

FEATHERS

As well as allowing most birds to fly, feathers keep them warm and dry. They come in all sorts of shapes and colors.
- Soft, down feathers are for warmth.
- Straight, strong feathers are for flying.
- Eye-catching feathers attract a mate.

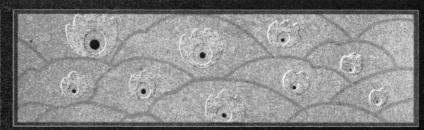

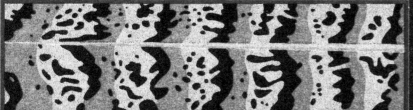

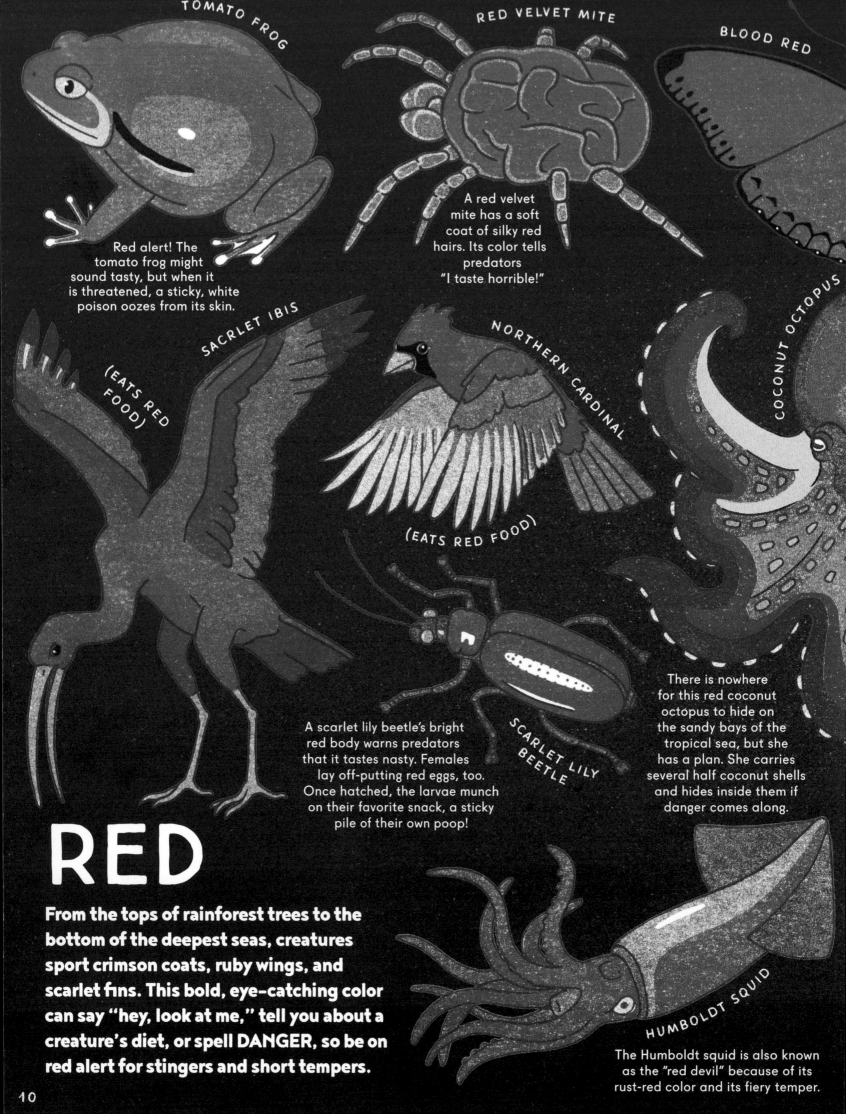

TOMATO FROG

Red alert! The tomato frog might sound tasty, but when it is threatened, a sticky, white poison oozes from its skin.

RED VELVET MITE

A red velvet mite has a soft coat of silky red hairs. Its color tells predators "I taste horrible!"

BLOOD RED

SACRLET IBIS

(EATS RED FOOD)

NORTHERN CARDINAL

(EATS RED FOOD)

COCONUT OCTOPUS

There is nowhere for this red coconut octopus to hide on the sandy bays of the tropical sea, but she has a plan. She carries several half coconut shells and hides inside them if danger comes along.

A scarlet lily beetle's bright red body warns predators that it tastes nasty. Females lay off-putting red eggs, too. Once hatched, the larvae munch on their favorite snack, a sticky pile of their own poop!

SCARLET LILY BEETLE

RED

From the tops of rainforest trees to the bottom of the deepest seas, creatures sport crimson coats, ruby wings, and scarlet fins. This bold, eye-catching color can say "hey, look at me," tell you about a creature's diet, or spell DANGER, so be on red alert for stingers and short tempers.

HUMBOLDT SQUID

The Humboldt squid is also known as the "red devil" because of its rust-red color and its fiery temper.

GLIDER BUTTERFLY

(CAMOUFLAGE)

RED VELVET ANT

(DANGER)

RED PANDA

The red panda spends its days sunbathing and snoozing in the treetops. Its red and cream coat blends in among the mossy branches of its forest home. At dusk it stretches, washes, and clambers down to chew on bamboo shoots.

RED SEA STAR

(DANGER)

CHRISTMAS ISLAND RED CRAB

SIAMESE FIGHTING FISH

In the wet season, Christmas Island red crabs emerge from their forest burrows and set off in their millions on a week-long trek to the coast to mate. Female crabs release their eggs into the ocean, before making the long trip home.

A male Siamese fighting fish hates rivals. He fans his flowing scarlet fins in a threatening fashion and tries to bite scales off an intruder until it swims away.

JAPANESE MACAQUE

RED RACER SNAKE (DANGER)

To Japanese macaques a rosy red face is a sign of good health and a pale face means an animal could be unwell.

ORANGE & PINK

MALE ORANGE-CLAWED FIDDLER CRAB

This crab creeps out of his burrow at low tide and waves his huge orange pincer in the air. It's a signal telling males to stay away and females to come over.

GUIANAN COCK-OF-THE-ROCK

The zingy feathers and crest of this male Guianan cock-of-the-rock are designed to impress the ladies. The males put on a dazzling display: strutting, calling, and preening. The females peck their favorite dancer on back!

(CAMOUFLAGE)

ORANGE BABOON TARANTULA

RED FOX

(CAMOUFLAGE)

CLOWNFISH

The clear, wide stripes of the clownfish help them spot their own kind against the bright colors of the reef.

GOLDEN LION TAMARIN

The brighter my orange mane, the healthier and more attractive to females I appear.

PINK RIVER DOLPHIN

Amazon river dolphins get their pretty pink color from the sunlight on their skin and the crabs and shrimps that they eat. When they get excited, they blush a deeper shade of pink, just like us!

NAKED MOLE RAT

A naked mole rat scurries along like a sausage on legs. It lives its whole life in the dark, underground, so it has no fur or pigment at all.

FLAMINGO

Feasting on shrimps gives the flamingo its colorful feathers. Even its skin and blood turn pink!

The candy-colors of this rosy maple moth trick predators into thinking it is poisonous.

(WARNING)

EDIBLE SEA URCHIN

ROSY MAPLE MOTH

AXOLOTL (LACK OF PIGMENT)

In nature, flashes of flaming pink and orange act like a flag to attract attention, and soft sunset shades can help wildlife blend in. But an animal's color is not always for disguise or display. Two of the animals here have turned the color of their favorite food, one is naked, and another just has sensitive skin!

A hippopotamus' pink tinge comes from the special red fluid it makes to protect its skin from the sun.

HIPPOPOTAMUS

YELLOW

In the animal world, being yellow doesn't always make you stand out—it just depends where you are. This sunny color flashes brightly against ocean blues and jungle greens, but if you want to blend in, hide among yellow fruits, flowers, or golden leaves and grasses.

GOLDEN LANGUR (CAMOUFLAGE)

BANANA SLUG

A slug is usually a first-rate supper for a frog or bird, but the yellow skin of the banana slug puts even the hungriest hunters off their meal.

MADAGASCAN MOON MOTH

INDIAN BULLFROG

For most of the year, this Indian bullfrog is a swampy green, but when the rainy season arrives, he transforms to attract a female. His skin turns a bright shade of lemon and the bulging sacks on his neck that make the "croak," blue.

EYELASH VIPER (DANGER)

A female Madagascan moon moth leaves her cocoon and waits for darkness when male moths set out in search of a mate. During the day her wings keep her hidden among the sun-dappled trees.

GOLDEN APPLE SNAIL
(LACK OF PIGMENT)

14

SLENDER MONGOOSE

A golden slender mongoose sneaks unseen among the yellow savanna grasses, on the prowl for its next meaty meal.

YELLOW SEAHORSE (CAMOUFLAGE)

NORTHERN YELLOW BAT

The brownish-yellow fur of the northern yellow bat makes it hard to spot among the dead fronds of the palm trees where it roosts.

This zingy fish is only bright yellow while the sun is out.

YELLOW TANG

(SHOWING OFF)

A yellow flower is the perfect hiding place for this goldenrod crab spider as it waits to turn a passing wasp into a snack.

YELLOW WARBLER

YELLOW-BELLIED SEA SNAKE

Beware! A yellow-bellied sea snake floats along the surface of the water. Its color warns hungry seals and seabirds of its deadly venom and disgusting taste.

GOLDENROD CRAB SPIDER

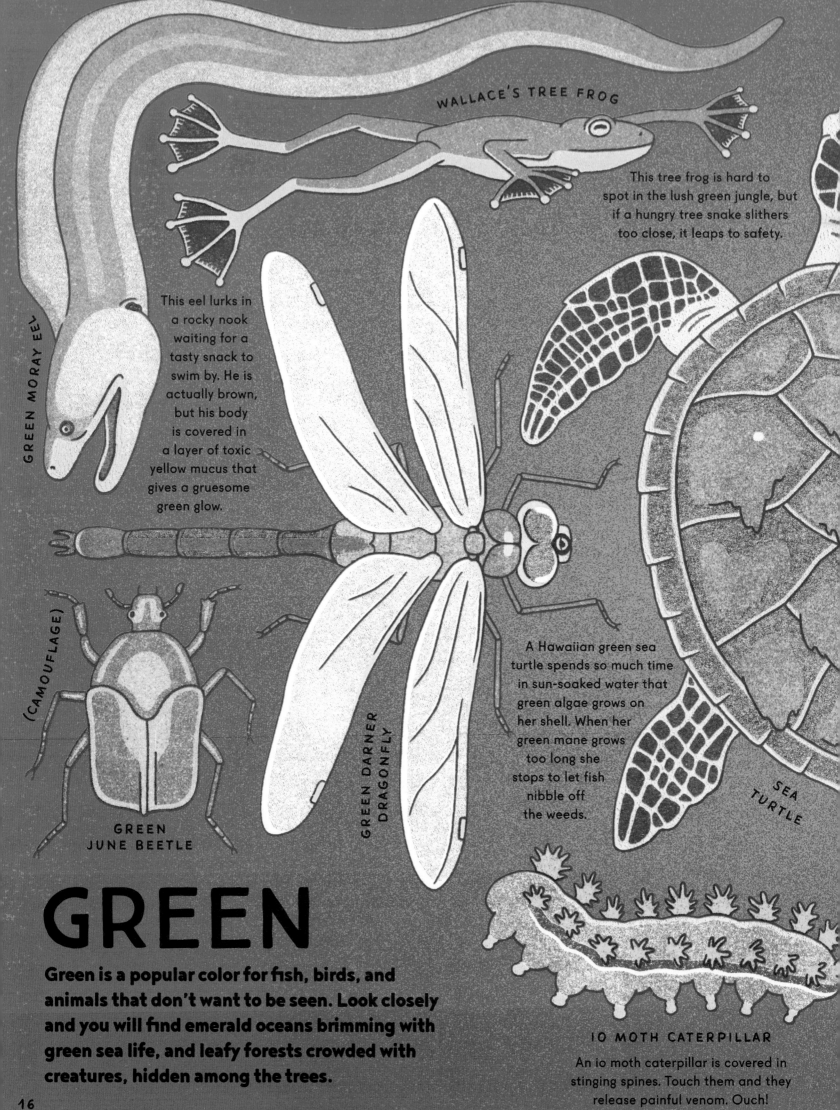

WALLACE'S TREE FROG

This tree frog is hard to spot in the lush green jungle, but if a hungry tree snake slithers too close, it leaps to safety.

GREEN MORAY EEL

This eel lurks in a rocky nook waiting for a tasty snack to swim by. He is actually brown, but his body is covered in a layer of toxic yellow mucus that gives a gruesome green glow.

(CAMOUFLAGE)

GREEN JUNE BEETLE

GREEN DARNER DRAGONFLY

A Hawaiian green sea turtle spends so much time in sun-soaked water that green algae grows on her shell. When her green mane grows too long she stops to let fish nibble off the weeds.

SEA TURTLE

GREEN

Green is a popular color for fish, birds, and animals that don't want to be seen. Look closely and you will find emerald oceans brimming with green sea life, and leafy forests crowded with creatures, hidden among the trees.

IO MOTH CATERPILLAR

An io moth caterpillar is covered in stinging spines. Touch them and they release painful venom. Ouch!

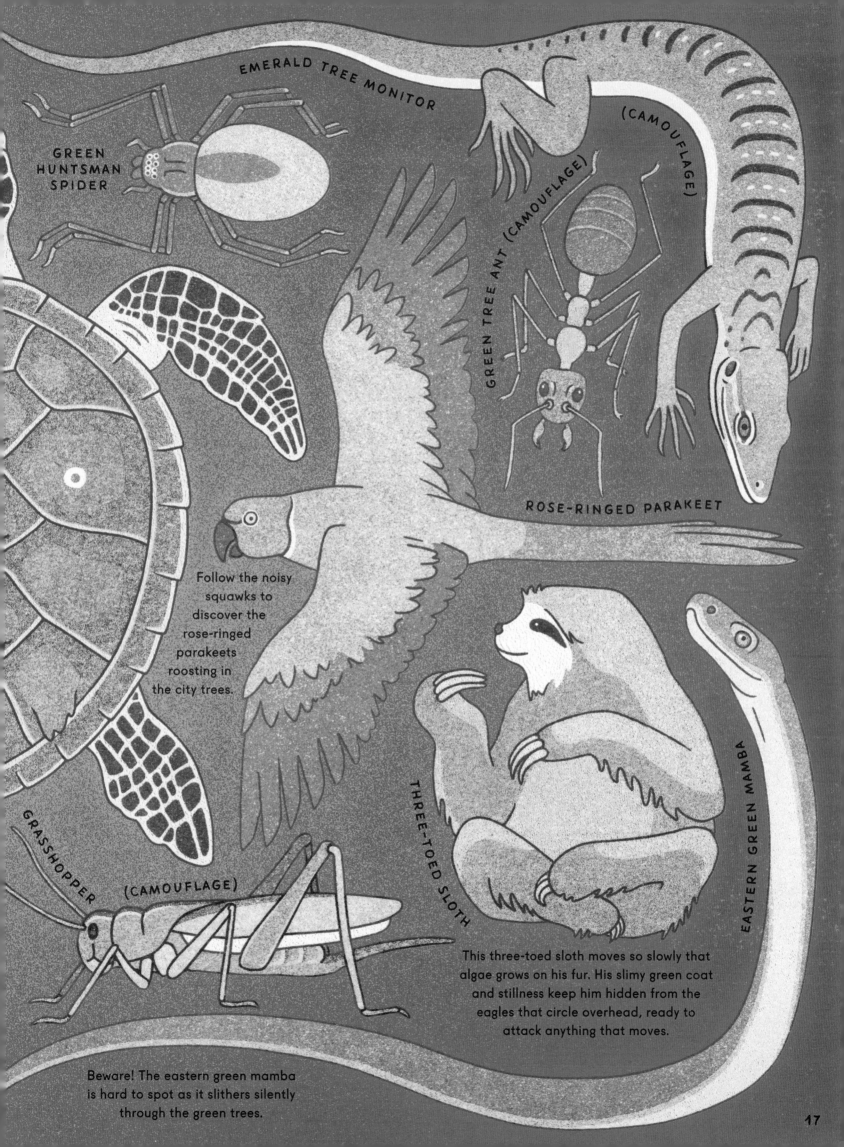

GREEN HUNTSMAN SPIDER

EMERALD TREE MONITOR

(CAMOUFLAGE)

GREEN TREE ANT (CAMOUFLAGE)

ROSE-RINGED PARAKEET

Follow the noisy squawks to discover the rose-ringed parakeets roosting in the city trees.

GRASSHOPPER

(CAMOUFLAGE)

THREE-TOED SLOTH

EASTERN GREEN MAMBA

This three-toed sloth moves so slowly that algae grows on his fur. His slimy green coat and stillness keep him hidden from the eagles that circle overhead, ready to attack anything that moves.

Beware! The eastern green mamba is hard to spot as it slithers silently through the green trees.

17

BLUE

Blue is everywhere in the animal world, from shimmering feathers and scales to sapphire tentacles and tails. There are even flashy turquoise feet! On land and in the sky, blue catches the eye, but in the ocean it helps hide you from hunters who wait to catch you out.

BLUE SHARK

The sleek back of a blue shark is hard to spot from above since it is the same color as the deep sea. From below its pale blue body blends with the sky.

HUMPHEAD WRASSE

(CAMOUFLAGE)

CARPATHIAN BLUE SLUG (DANGER)

BLUE-TAILED SKINK

The male satin bowerbird collects all things blue, from feathers, forks, and petals to plastic bottle tops. He scatters them on the floor of his stick bower and struts around with his blue treasure in his beak, hoping to charm a female.

SATIN BOWERBIRD

A blue-tailed skink is an expert escape artist. When attacked, it disconnects its eye-catching tail, leaving it twitching in the mouth of a surprised snake or bird. The skink runs to safety and soon grows a new blue tail.

There's a blue flash as a blue morpho butterfly flutters through the jungle. Tiny scales on her wings reflect the light, making them shimmer. She lands and closes her wings to reveal the brown underside and is hidden.

BLUE MORPHO BUTTERFLY

KINGFISHER

Turquoise feathers flash as a kingfisher dives head first into a stream. Just like the morpho butterfly, its feathers are actually brown but bounce back blue light.

ELECTRIC BLUE GECKO

Only the male electric blue gecko is this glimmering turquoise to attract an admiring female.

GRAND CAYMAN BLUE IGUANA

MAN-O-WAR

LITTLE BLUE HERON (CAMOUFLAGE)

The huge and deadly Portuguese man-o-war is an inky blue to blend in with the deep sea. It has a balloon-like float that stays on the surface of the water and catches the wind and moves it along.

BLUE-FOOTED BOOBY

A blue-footed booby waddles along the shore of his Galapagos-island home. He proudly lifts up his startling blue feet one by one for a passing female to admire. She shows she is impressed by copying his fancy footwork.

This sky-blue male mountain bluebird bird can be seen easily by females who admire his azure allure.

MOUNTAIN BLUEBIRD

19

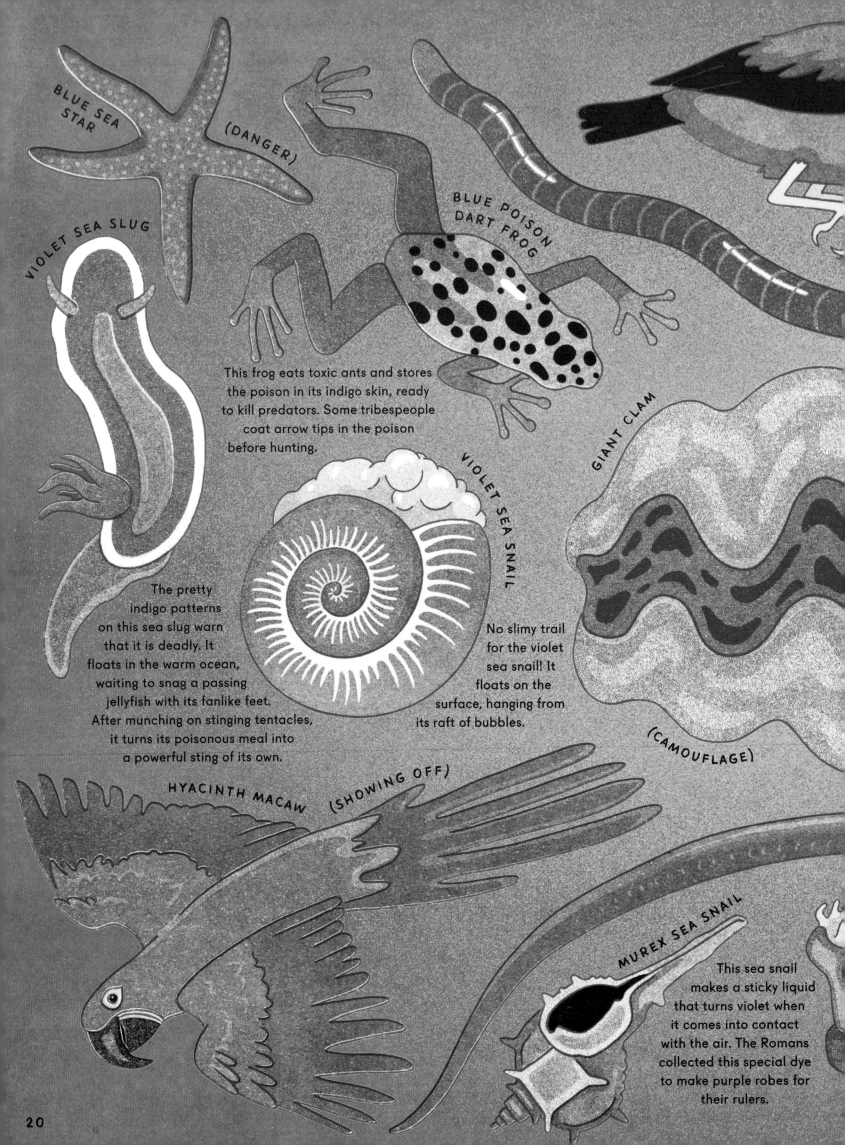

BLUE SEA STAR

(DANGER)

VIOLET SEA SLUG

BLUE POISON DART FROG

This frog eats toxic ants and stores the poison in its indigo skin, ready to kill predators. Some tribespeople coat arrow tips in the poison before hunting.

GIANT CLAM

VIOLET SEA SNAIL

The pretty indigo patterns on this sea slug warn that it is deadly. It floats in the warm ocean, waiting to snag a passing jellyfish with its fanlike feet. After munching on stinging tentacles, it turns its poisonous meal into a powerful sting of its own.

No slimy trail for the violet sea snail! It floats on the surface, hanging from its raft of bubbles.

(CAMOUFLAGE)

HYACINTH MACAW   (SHOWING OFF)

MUREX SEA SNAIL

This sea snail makes a sticky liquid that turns violet when it comes into contact with the air. The Romans collected this special dye to make purple robes for their rulers.

PURPLE HONEY CREEPER

(SHOWING OFF)

BOETTGER'S CAECILIAN

BIRD OF PARADISE

This wormlike creature's slimy skin oozes poison that harms hungry attackers.

This male blue bird of paradise hangs upside down from a branch, spreads his incredible indigo-tipped feathers, and flutters them at the females.

(CAMOUFLAGE)

BLUE CRAB

PACIFIC WARTY OCTOPUS
Deep in the Pacific Ocean a little purple octopus feels with its suckers for worms and snails hiding in the mud.

EASTERN INDIGO SNAKE (STAYING HIDDEN)

MAGNIFICENT SEA ANEMONE (DANGER)

INDIGO & VIOLET

You have to hunt high and low to find violet and indigo animals. They are fanning their feathers up in the trees, croaking and hopping under the leaves, slithering and burrowing above and below ground, and some are wriggling at the bottom of the sea.

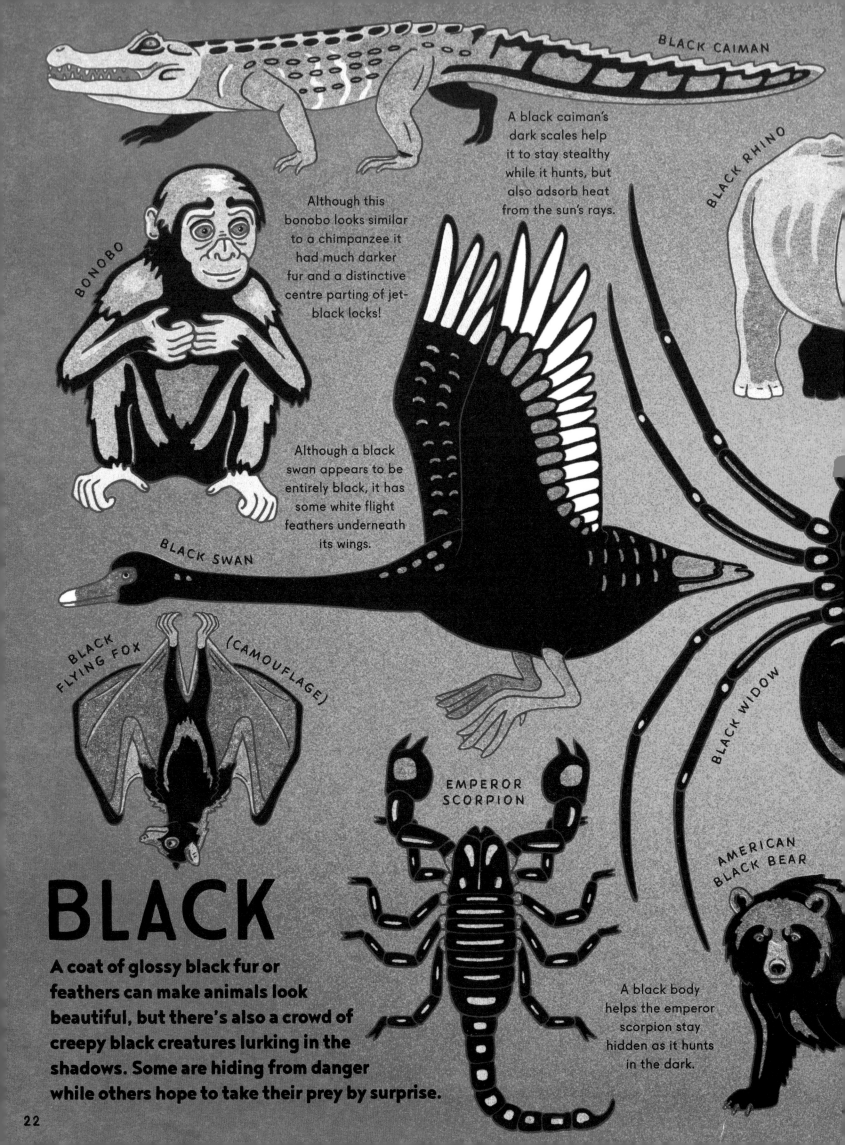

BLACK CAIMAN

A black caiman's dark scales help it to stay stealthy while it hunts, but also adsorb heat from the sun's rays.

BLACK RHINO

BONOBO

Although this bonobo looks similar to a chimpanzee it had much darker fur and a distinctive centre parting of jet-black locks!

Although a black swan appears to be entirely black, it has some white flight feathers underneath its wings.

BLACK SWAN

BLACK FLYING FOX

(CAMOUFLAGE)

BLACK WIDOW

EMPEROR SCORPION

AMERICAN BLACK BEAR

BLACK

A coat of glossy black fur or feathers can make animals look beautiful, but there's also a crowd of creepy black creatures lurking in the shadows. Some are hiding from danger while others hope to take their prey by surprise.

A black body helps the emperor scorpion stay hidden as it hunts in the dark.

Black rhinos are really gray. They look black because they cover themselves in thick, dark mud.

A dung beetle's black body helps it emit heat in the hot desert. Water vapor coming off its ball of poop also keeps it cool!

DUNG BEETLE

AYAM CEMANI CHICKEN

This Ayam cemani chicken looks very stylish, strutting around with his glossy ebony feathers. Every part of him is black, from the top of his comb to the tip of his scaly toes. His skin, organs, flesh, and bones are jet-black, too!

GIANT AFRICAN MILLIPEDE

(DANGER)

RAVEN

The raven's dark feather's absorb and trap the sun's heat.

The small but deadly black widow spider waits in a dark corner for something tasty to get tangled in her web.

(CAMOUFLAGE)

BLACK PANTHER

EUROPEAN MOLE (CAMOUFLAGE)

Any black wildcat is known as a black panther. These jet-black jaguars and leopards are born with extra melanin—the stuff that makes skin and fur dark. Their inky coats hide them as they slink through the dark jungle to hunt at nighttime.

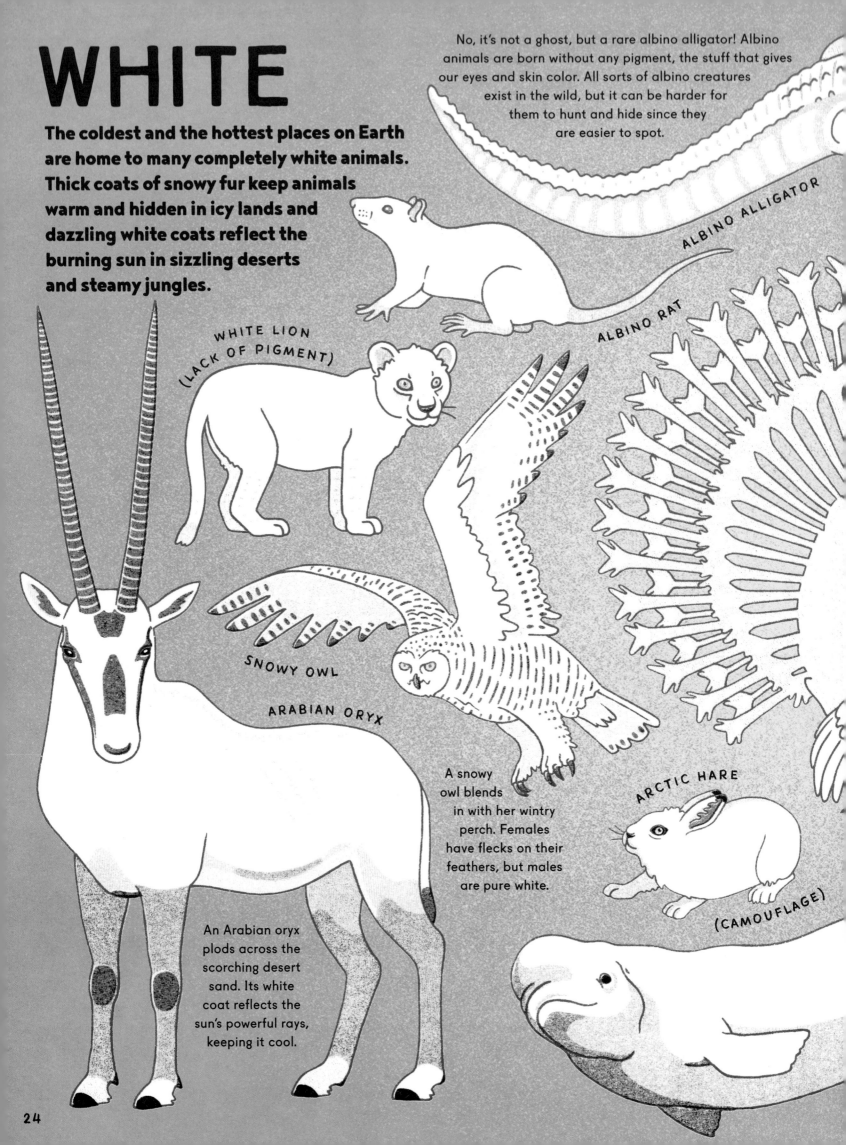

WHITE

The coldest and the hottest places on Earth are home to many completely white animals. Thick coats of snowy fur keep animals warm and hidden in icy lands and dazzling white coats reflect the burning sun in sizzling deserts and steamy jungles.

No, it's not a ghost, but a rare albino alligator! Albino animals are born without any pigment, the stuff that gives our eyes and skin color. All sorts of albino creatures exist in the wild, but it can be harder for them to hunt and hide since they are easier to spot.

ALBINO ALLIGATOR

ALBINO RAT

WHITE LION
(LACK OF PIGMENT)

SNOWY OWL

ARABIAN ORYX

A snowy owl blends in with her wintry perch. Females have flecks on their feathers, but males are pure white.

ARCTIC HARE

(CAMOUFLAGE)

An Arabian oryx plods across the scorching desert sand. Its white coat reflects the sun's powerful rays, keeping it cool.

This spirit bear has come out of the forest to hunt for salmon. She is one of about 400 North American bears with white fur. Her creamy coat blends with the bright sky, so she is able to snatch a fish supper before the salmon notice her looming overhead.

SPIRIT BEAR

CUBAN TREE FROG

(SHOWING OFF)

ALBINO PEACOCK

SULPHUR-CRESTED COCKATOO

When nestling under a leaf this bat looks just like a wasp nest so hungry creatures don't eat it.

BELUGA WHALE

HONDURAN WHITE BAT

ARCTIC WOLF

An Arctic wolf prowls through the frozen forest. Thick fur even protects his paws and helps him to grip the icy surface.

This beluga whale's snowy skin helps keep her hidden from hungry polar bears and killer whales lurking above and below the Arctic ice.

25

MARBLED SALAMANDER

To a passing bird, the eye-catching marbled salamander sends a monochrome danger message! This juicy snack is packed with poison.

EMPEROR PENGUIN

This emperor penguin and its chick live in the cold Antarctic. They may have black heads and backs to help them soak up the sun's heat. They are white underneath so that as they swim fish don't spot them against the white sky. above.

BLACK-NECKED SWAN

The rare black-necked swan has a very chic color scheme. The male and females both have a red fleshy bulge on their beak, but the male's is much larger and shows that it is a good mate.

The bald-faced hornet is actually a type of wasp. Its pale rear may look less like a danger warning than bright yellow cousins but its sting is much more painful.

BALD-FACED HORNET

CALIFORNIA KINGSNAKE

This snake's striking stripes may help to ward off predators, who might mistake it for one of its more poisonous distant cousins!

This tamarin monkey has an unusual white moustache. It earned itself the name "emperor" after a German ruler who sported similarly magnificent facial hair!

EMPEROR TAMARIN

DOMINO BEETLE (DANGER)

BLACK & WHITE

Why are so many animals black and white? To our eyes, this dazzling combo seems like a bad idea for creatures trying to survive in the wild. But light and dark stripes, patches, bands, and spikes can help animals look scary, keep warm, change shape, and even disappear in plain sight!

A puffin's black back absorbs warm sun. its white chest feathers do a similar job to a penguin's.

PUFFIN

WHITE TIGER

Every tiger has a different pattern of stripes—a bit like a person's unique fingerprints. But a white tiger is particularly unusual and extremely rare in the wild. Many people have written stories about how magical they look.

INYO TOAD

EASTERN GARTER SNAKE

An inyo toad's clever pattern helps it to blend in among dark leaf mulch and pools of light-dappled water on the forest floor.

This sleek, chic snake with a go-faster stripe looks deadly poisonous. But don't be fooled, it is nonvenomous and mostly dines on frogs and worms.

RAINBOW

These bright creatures look like they come from a fantasy coloring book. Beaks and bodies are splashed with yellow and green, and shells and scales are shaded with orange and red. One animal has even been given a colorful face and behind!

RED-SIDED GARTER SNAKE
(DANGER)

KEEL-BILLED TOUCAN

Scientists are unsure whether a toucan's bright beak is to warn predators away or to help them blend into the bright and colorful jungle.

CUBAN LAND SNAIL

Cuban land snails look like they have colored in their own swirly shells. When choosing a slimy mate, they circle each other VERY slowly, checking out each other's paintwork.

RAINBOW GRASSHOPPER

ELEGANT GOLDEN JUMPING SPIDER

Which of its colorful names suits this shellfish best—the clown, harlequin, rainbow, or peacock mantis shrimp?

(DANGER)

The cheerful colors of the rainbow grasshopper warn birds that it tastes revolting.

PEACOCK MANTIS SHRIMP

CORTEZ RAINBOW WRASSE

(DANGER)

BROADLEY'S FLAT LIZARD

Meet the world's most colorful monkey! The male mandrill is topped and tailed with a blue and red face and behind. It's a look that female mandrills can't resist!

MANDRILL

(DANGER)

CUCKOO WASP

RED-EYED TREE FROG

If a sleeping red-eyed tree frog is disturbed, it stuns the intruder by flashing its bulging red eyes and bright markings. This buys the frog a few seconds in which to leap to safety.

(DANGER)

(SHOWING OFF)

RAINBOW LORIKEET

INDIAN GIANT SQUIRREL

The Indian giant squirrel may look like it has been tie-dyed, but its maroon and purple fur blends in beautifully with the sun-flecked forest. To hide, the squirrel just flattens itself against a tree.

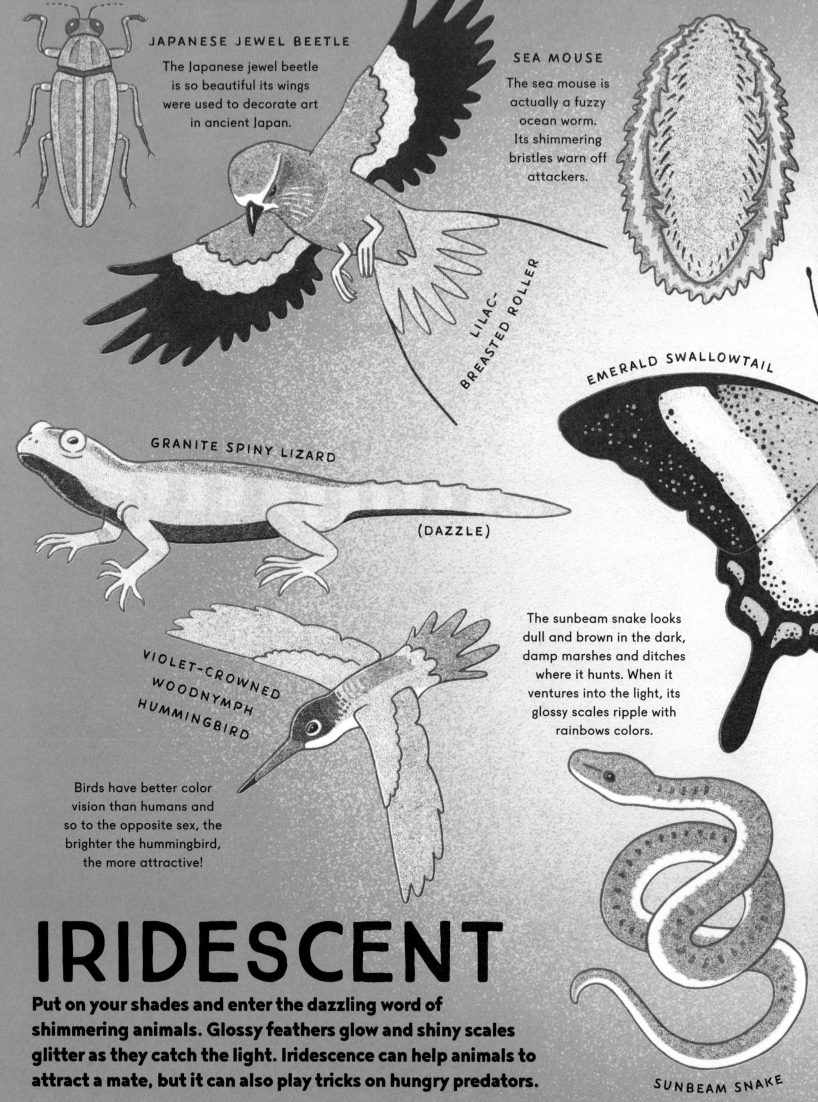

JAPANESE JEWEL BEETLE

The Japanese jewel beetle is so beautiful its wings were used to decorate art in ancient Japan.

SEA MOUSE

The sea mouse is actually a fuzzy ocean worm. Its shimmering bristles warn off attackers.

LILAC-BREASTED ROLLER

EMERALD SWALLOWTAIL

GRANITE SPINY LIZARD

(DAZZLE)

The sunbeam snake looks dull and brown in the dark, damp marshes and ditches where it hunts. When it ventures into the light, its glossy scales ripple with rainbows colors.

VIOLET-CROWNED WOODNYMPH HUMMINGBIRD

Birds have better color vision than humans and so to the opposite sex, the brighter the hummingbird, the more attractive!

IRIDESCENT

Put on your shades and enter the dazzling word of shimmering animals. Glossy feathers glow and shiny scales glitter as they catch the light. Iridescence can help animals to attract a mate, but it can also play tricks on hungry predators.

SUNBEAM SNAKE

BLIND GOLDEN MOLE

The only animal on Earth with iridescent fur lives underground. Scientists think that the blind golden mole has super silky hair to help it slip smoothly through tight tunnels—it just happens to be iridescent as well!

The reflective feathers of the greater blue-eared starling make it gleam like polished metal.

GREATER BLUE-EARED STARLING

Like many butterflies, the emerald swallowtail has dazzling iridescent wings. Tiny mirrorlike scales on the wings scatter the light and make them shimmer. This clever trick can confuse hungry birds.

The shark catfish is also known as the iridescent shark because of its sleek shape and pearly glow.

SHARK CATFISH

Perched on a rock, the male sarada superba lizard blends perfectly in, then he arches his back and puffs up his glittering throat flap. His aim is to scare off rival males and win over a lady.

NICOBAR PIGEON

The orchid bee looks almost metallic. Some scientists think this helps it to disguise itself as a droplet of water inside a flower.

ORCHID BEE

SARADA SUPERBA LIZARD

(SHOWING OFF)

This bright bird is the closest living relative to the extinct dodo. Its shaggy and dazzling iridescent feathers help it to attract a mate.

STRIPES

When you think of stripes you might just see zebras. But bugs, mammals, birds, and fish the world over have stripes on their legs, wings, bodies, and streaked through their manes. They are all striped for different reasons. Most often stripes help an animal blend into its surroundings or camouflage itself but sometimes they have evolved streaks for other more unusual reasons.

(CAMOUFLAGE)

STRIPED GRASS MOUSE

APOLLO METALMARK BUTTERFLY

BLUE SEA SLUG

(DANGER)

TABBY CAT (CAMOUFLAGE)

If a fish lives alone and not in a school it is more likely to have stripes. Big groups of fish dazzle their predators by darting around and finding safety in numbers. This little stripy fish keeps a low profile amid the seagrass, its patterned body making hungry passersby confuse it for weeds.

STRIPED BURRFISH

TIGER (CAMOUFLAGE)

The European striped shield bug looks like a cinnamon candy but its stripes are a danger sign to any creatures in search of a snack. As well as the warning stripes, if an animal gets too close, the bug lets out a foul-smelling liquid made from poisonous cyanide.

EASTERN STRIPED CRICKET

(DANGER)

(DAZZLE)

MONARCH CATERPILLAR

(DANGER)

RING-TAILED LEMUR

A lemur raises its striped tail when it sees danger.

(CAMOUFLAGE)

RED-BELLIED WOODPECKER

(DANGER)

ANNA'S CHROMODORIS SEA SLUG

ZEBRA

EUROPEAN STRIPED SHIELD BUG

MOUNTAIN BONGO

(CAMOUFLAGE)

The zebra is an A-lister in the world of stripes. Scientists thought for a long time that a zebra's stripes were there to help it blend into the grasslands. Now people think that they are there to confuse flies who don't see the stripy creature as something solid to land on.

(DANGER)

NEMBROTHA AUREA SEA SLUG

33

SPOTS

Are you seeing dots before your eyes? Wildlife sends out a warning with spots or uses patches to disappear into the shadows. Speckles and spots can help scientists too. They study animals' patterns to tell creatures apart, or to work out their age.

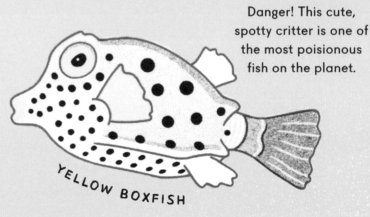

Danger! This cute, spotty critter is one of the most poisionous fish on the planet.

YELLOW BOXFISH

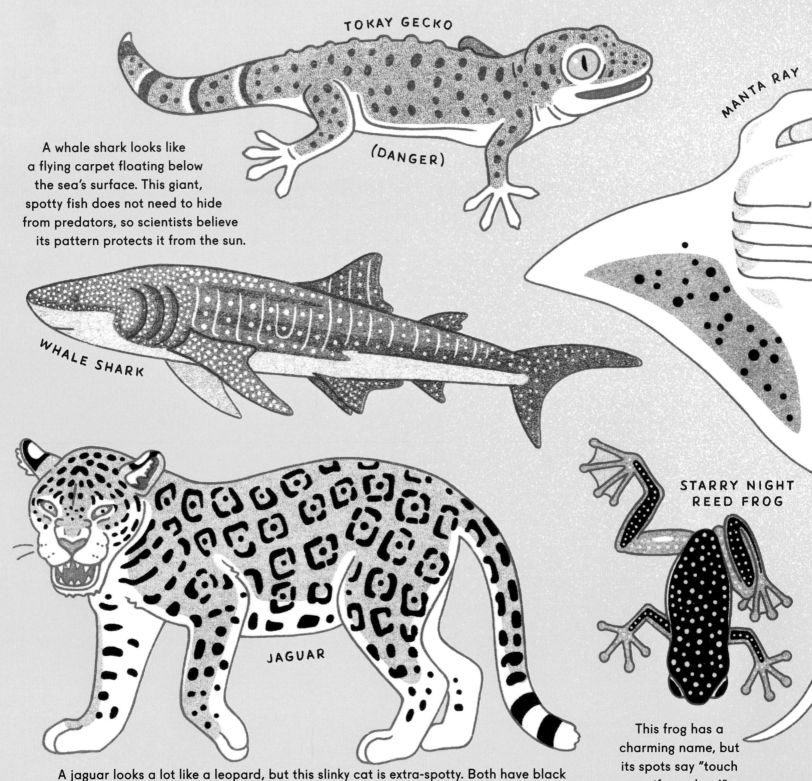

TOKAY GECKO

(DANGER)

A whale shark looks like a flying carpet floating below the sea's surface. This giant, spotty fish does not need to hide from predators, so scientists believe its pattern protects it from the sun.

WHALE SHARK

MANTA RAY

STARRY NIGHT REED FROG

JAGUAR

A jaguar looks a lot like a leopard, but this slinky cat is extra-spotty. Both have black rings, but only the jaguar's are filled with dots. Now you can spot the difference!

This frog has a charming name, but its spots say "touch me if you dare!"

SPOTTED TURTLE

This spotted turtle is peppered with polka dots. The older the turtle, the more spots it has.

CLOWN TRIGGERFISH

(DANGER)

Each manta ray is born with a different set of blotches on its belly. Even identical twin pups have their own unique pattern of patches. Scientists use the spots to identify every manta ray they see.

EASTERN QUOLL

(CAMOUFLAGE)

UPSIDE-DOWN CATFISH

An upside-down catfish swims belly-up along the surface of rivers and lakes, feeding on flies that land on the water. Its speckled scales hide it from threats both above and below the water.

(DANGER)

DOMINO BEETLE

GIRAFFE

The paving-stone patches on a giraffe help it to hide in dappled light. They also keep it cool. Lots of tiny blood vessels under each dark shape allow heat to escape through the giraffe's skin.

CHANGING COLOR

Some creatures can switch colors in the blink of an eye, to hide from danger, or to flash a warning. Some slowly change to match the seasons, and other, normally plain, animals strut their stuff with eye-popping looks just once a year.

VEILED CHAMELEON (AGGRESSIVE)

(AGGRESSIVE)

GOLDEN TORTOISE BEETLE

ERMINE (WINTER)

(SUMMER)

(ON A PALE BACKGROUND)

MALE GORILLA (ADULT)

PUFFIN

DWARF CUTTLEFISH

The dwarf cuttlefish can change its color to match a new background in the blink of an eye.

ARCTIC FOX

GREEN IGUANA

(MATING SEASON)

PEACOCK FLOUNDER

(WINTER)

(CALM)

(CALM)

Chameleons show their feelings through their skin. Male veiled chameleons even settle quarrels with colors. A bright pattern means "Back off!" and turning pale means "You win."

This glitzy golden tortoise beetle warns off attackers by quickly turning its wings bright red.

Male gorillas change from "blackbacks" to "silverbacks" when they are about twelve years old. Their new silvery hair shows that they are fully grown—like teenage boys sprouting beards and moustaches.

ERMINE (SUMMER)

(WINTER)

(YOUNG)

(ON A DARK BACKGROUND)

In spring, puffins sport amazing multicolored beaks and matching orange feet to attract a mate. By winter they look so faded and drab that scientists used to think they were a different breed of bird!

DWARF CUTTLEFISH

In winter, an Arctic fox blends in perfectly with its frosty habitat. In spring, it sheds its snowy white coat for earthy colors and blends in again.

ARCTIC FOX

GREEN IGUANA

Wherever a peacock flounder settles on the seabed, its cool color-changing skin can match its background in seconds, making it almost invisible. It can even copy the checks on a chessboard. Beat that!

(SPRING)

Green iguanas turn carrot-colored when it's time to pick a mate. That way they can't miss each other!

STAND OUT

Meet some of nature's biggest show-offs. They have eye-catching feathers, shimmering fins, and beautiful behinds in a rainbow of colors. Some animals prefer to blend in and have just one stand-out trademark to confuse predators or to help them communicate with their own kind.

PEACOCK SPIDER

Over here! A peacock spider waves its beautiful behind to attract a female.

GREEN ANOLE

Not only does this type of chameleon have a magnificent strawberry-colored throat but it can change color at the drop of a hat!

RABBIT

A fox or hawk chasing a rabbit fixes on its bobbing white tail. When the rabbit darts to the side, its tail disappears, confusing the hunter and giving the bunny a chance to bolt down a burrow.

RED-LIPPED BATFISH

KERAMA DEER

When a male peafowl, or peacock, fans out his fabulous feathers, over 160 eye spots shimmer around his elegant head. The females, called peahens, pick the males with the most spectacular tails.

Kerama deer flag danger to the herd by signalling with their white tails.

Pucker up for the pouting red-lipped batfish! The ruby lips of these ocean-floor-dwelling sea creatures may help them to find eachother in the dark.

PEACOCK

38

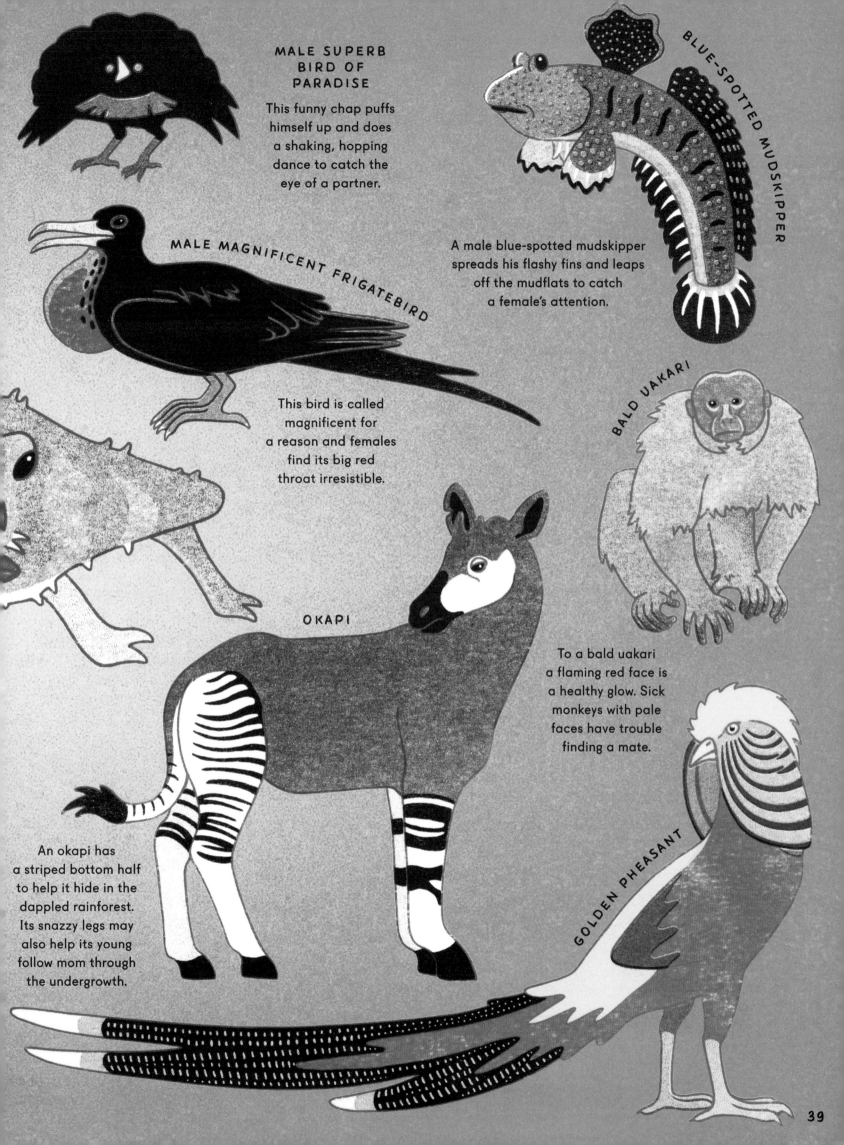

MALE SUPERB BIRD OF PARADISE

This funny chap puffs himself up and does a shaking, hopping dance to catch the eye of a partner.

BLUE-SPOTTED MUDSKIPPER

A male blue-spotted mudskipper spreads his flashy fins and leaps off the mudflats to catch a female's attention.

MALE MAGNIFICENT FRIGATEBIRD

This bird is called magnificent for a reason and females find its big red throat irresistible.

BALD UAKARI

To a bald uakari a flaming red face is a healthy glow. Sick monkeys with pale faces have trouble finding a mate.

OKAPI

An okapi has a striped bottom half to help it hide in the dappled rainforest. Its snazzy legs may also help its young follow mom through the undergrowth.

GOLDEN PHEASANT

VIETNAMESE MOSSY FROG

Camouflaged in her golden coat, a lioness can slink through the dry grass unnoticed.

LIONESS

VINE SNAKE

NIGHTJAR

A nightjar's tawny colored feathers and ability to stay absolutely still make it look just like the rock or branch it perches on. Its prey has no idea they are being watched...

AFRICAN WILD DOG

WRAP-AROUND SPIDER

The teeny wrap-around spider flattens its body and hugs branches to blend in with the bark.

Just before dawn, an African wild dog pricks up its big, round ears and listens out for prey. The black and tan blotches on its coat make it disappear into the grassy plains as it hunts in the faint light.

A polar bear has a thick, white coat to keep it cosy and camouflaged in the Arctic snow and ice. Under its fur, its skin is black to soak up the sun's warmth.

POLAR BEAR

MOSSY LEAF-TAILED GECKO

PEPPERED MOTH

A tasselled wobbegong shark waits patiently on the coral. Its speckled skin makes it invisible to unsuspecting fish.

TASSELLED WOBBEGONG SHARK

BLEND IN

Ready for some conjuring tricks? Clever camouflage can make snakes disappear, birds vanish, and big cats fade away as if by magic. For the hunters, their colors and patterns help them to grab a meal, and for the hunted, blending in is a lifesaver.

COPPERHEAD SNAKE

Is it a branch or a bird? The potoo sleeps still and upright, blending in with its wooden perch.

POTOO

SPOTTED HYENA

A young copperhead snake lies very still, its earthy colored stripes merging into the leaves that litter the ground. It twitches its yellow-tipped tail to tempt birds and lizard looking for a juicy worm.

The flashy chrysalis of the orange-spotted tiger clearwing butterfly seems a bad choice for a creature trying to hide, but its mirrored home plays tricks on predators. It can be mistaken for a drop of water, a shaft of light, or a dry, curled leaf.

SNOW LEOPARD

ORANGE-SPOTTED TIGER CLEARWING BUTTERFLY CHRYSALIS

FIRE-BELLIED TOAD

LOWLAND STREAKED TENREC

Don't mess with a lowland streaked tenrec. It springs headfirst at its foe with sharp yellow spikes raised, ready to pierce skin with its hard hair spikes.

Strike a pose! The toxic rough-skinned newt flashes its yellow underbelly.

ROUGH-SKINNED NEWT

Yikes, it's a lion fish. Look at those venomous spikes! Nothing tells predators "don't touch me" quite like this beautiful but deadly display.

SKUNK

When a skunk raises its tail, it's time to run! The black-and-white stripe is a sign. Ignore it and the skunk will turn and squirt a stinking liquid from its behind.

STRIPED PYJAMA SQUID

POISONOUS PUSS MOTH CATERPILLAR

Steer clear of the poisonous puss moth caterpillar. It waves its warning tails and lifts its alarming head, ringed with red like a gaping mouth.

WARN OFF

Animals communicate in a colorful language that helps to keep them safe. Learn to read the signs written in spots and stripes, and the warning colors of red, yellow, black, and white. They tell of foul tastes, fierce fangs, lethal poisons, and deadly spikes.

FIRE SALAMANDER

The toxic-looking fire salamander is not bluffing—it is covered from nose to tail in deadly poison.

DEADLY BLUE-RINGED OCTOPUS

The small but deadly blue-ringed octopus packs enough poison to kill within minutes. Bright blue rings appear on its body to warn predators that this lunch is lethal.

PSYCHEDELIC MANDARIN FISH

Warning: this psychedelic mandarin fish has poisonous slime AND a foul smell—and it's not afraid to use them.

LION FISH

AMERICAN BADGER

The stripes on the American badger lead to the source of danger—its menacing mouth! Its jaw is very strong and it is not shy to defend itself.

BLUE KRAIT

A highly venomous snake whose stripes gives predators ample warning.

STINGING ROSE MOTH CATERPILLAR

SPINX MOTH CATERPILLAR

A sphinx moth caterpillar has a cool survival trick. It dangles from a twig to reveal fake snake skin and shining eyespots. It then inflates its head to complete its disguise as a deadly viper.

MIMIC OCTOPUS (HARMLESS)

The mimic octopus can morph into a host of deadly sea creatures to stay safe. By arranging its legs and swimming in different styles it can copy a toxic flat fish, a spiky lion fish, and a poisonous sea snake.

SCARLET KINGSNAKE (HARMLESS)

WASP

JUMPING SPIDER

METALMARK MOTH

If you squint, the eye spots and leglike markings on this metalmark moth transform into a jumping spider. Most spiders that come across the moth think they have met a mate, not their lunch!

HOVERFLY

The harmless hoverfly is disguised as a stinging wasp.

When is an ant not an ant? When it's a kerengga ant-like jumper! This spider holds up her front legs to look like ant feelers and mixes unnoticed with her favorite snack— weaver ants!

COMMON MORMON BUTTERFLY (TASTY)

Would you confuse the ladybird mimic spider for the real, bad-tasting beetle?

WEAVER ANT

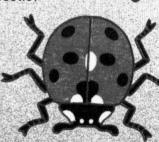

LADYBUG

FAKING IT

Keep your eyes peeled or you could be tricked by clever copycats and animal imposters. Watch out for fake eyes on ears, tails, behinds, and wings. Spot helpless creatures disguised to put off predators and beware of sneaky hunters imitating the animals they like to eat!

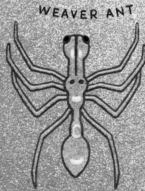

KERENGGA ANT-LIKE JUMPER

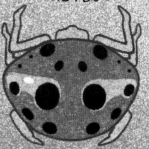

LADYBIRD MIMIC SPIDER

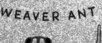

DEADLY VIPER

CORAL REEF SNAKE (VENOMOUS AND DEADLY)

EASTERN CORAL SNAKE (VENOMOUS AND DEADLY)

FALSE EYES

COMMON ROSE BUTTERFLY (BAD-TASTING)

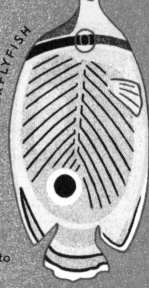

BUTTERFLYFISH

The eye spot on the butterflyfish fools predators into attacking its tail instead of its head.

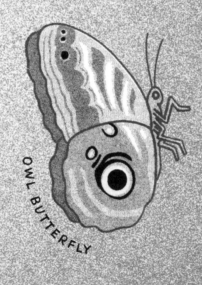

OWL BUTTERFLY

The northern pygmy owl seems to have eyes in the back of its head. Its fake eyes look a lot bigger than its real ones and make others think it is bigger and more fearsome.

A serval cat has eyelike markings called "ocille" on the back of its ears to scare away predators. The marks are so bold, cubs use them to keep sight of their parents in long grass.

NORTHERN PYGMY OWL

CUYABA DWARF FROG

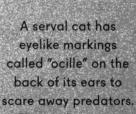

Yikes! The cuyaba dwarf frog has an inflatable, poisonous big-eyed behind!

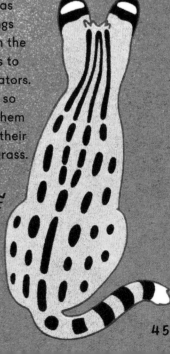

SERVAL

CLEVER DISGUISES

These plants and objects could leap into life at any moment. There are sticks that walk, leaves that fly, flowers that pounce, and logs that bite. That's because they are all animals in disguise, waiting to ambush prey, or hiding from hungry predators.

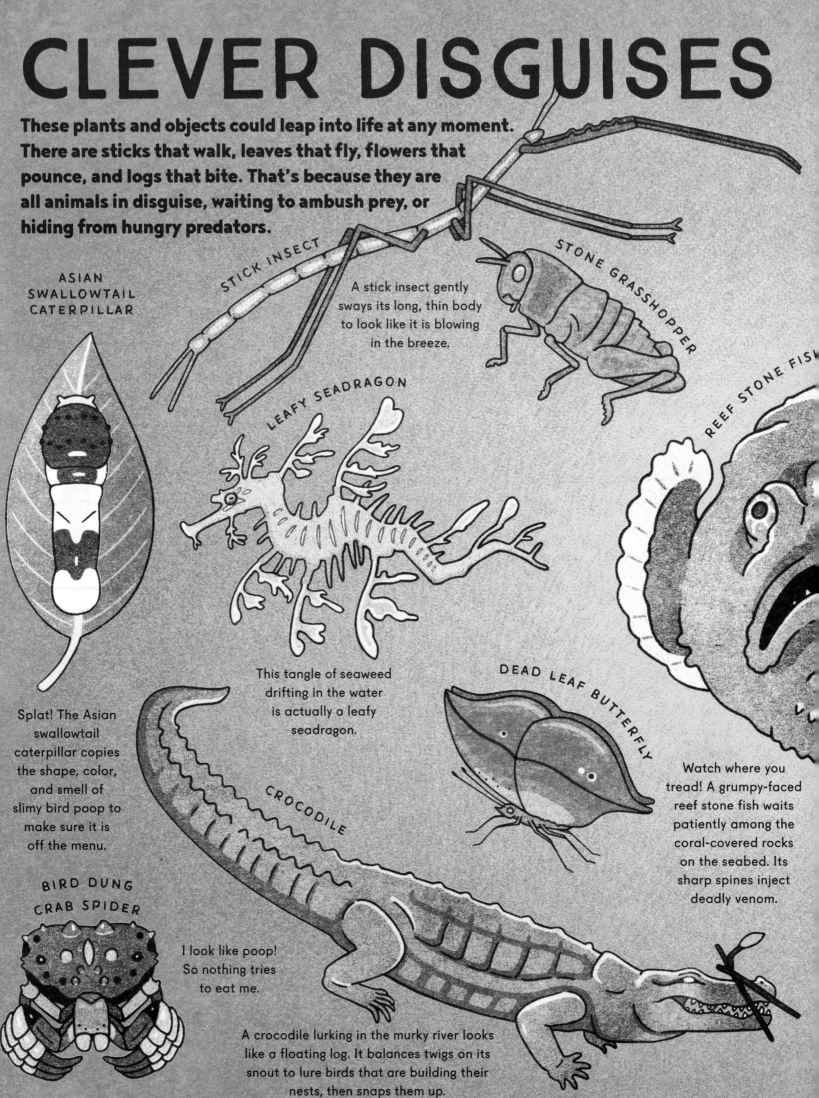

STICK INSECT

STONE GRASSHOPPER

ASIAN SWALLOWTAIL CATERPILLAR

A stick insect gently sways its long, thin body to look like it is blowing in the breeze.

LEAFY SEADRAGON

REEF STONE FISH

This tangle of seaweed drifting in the water is actually a leafy seadragon.

DEAD LEAF BUTTERFLY

Splat! The Asian swallowtail caterpillar copies the shape, color, and smell of slimy bird poop to make sure it is off the menu.

CROCODILE

Watch where you tread! A grumpy-faced reef stone fish waits patiently among the coral-covered rocks on the seabed. Its sharp spines inject deadly venom.

BIRD DUNG CRAB SPIDER

I look like poop! So nothing tries to eat me.

A crocodile lurking in the murky river looks like a floating log. It balances twigs on its snout to lure birds that are building their nests, then snaps them up.

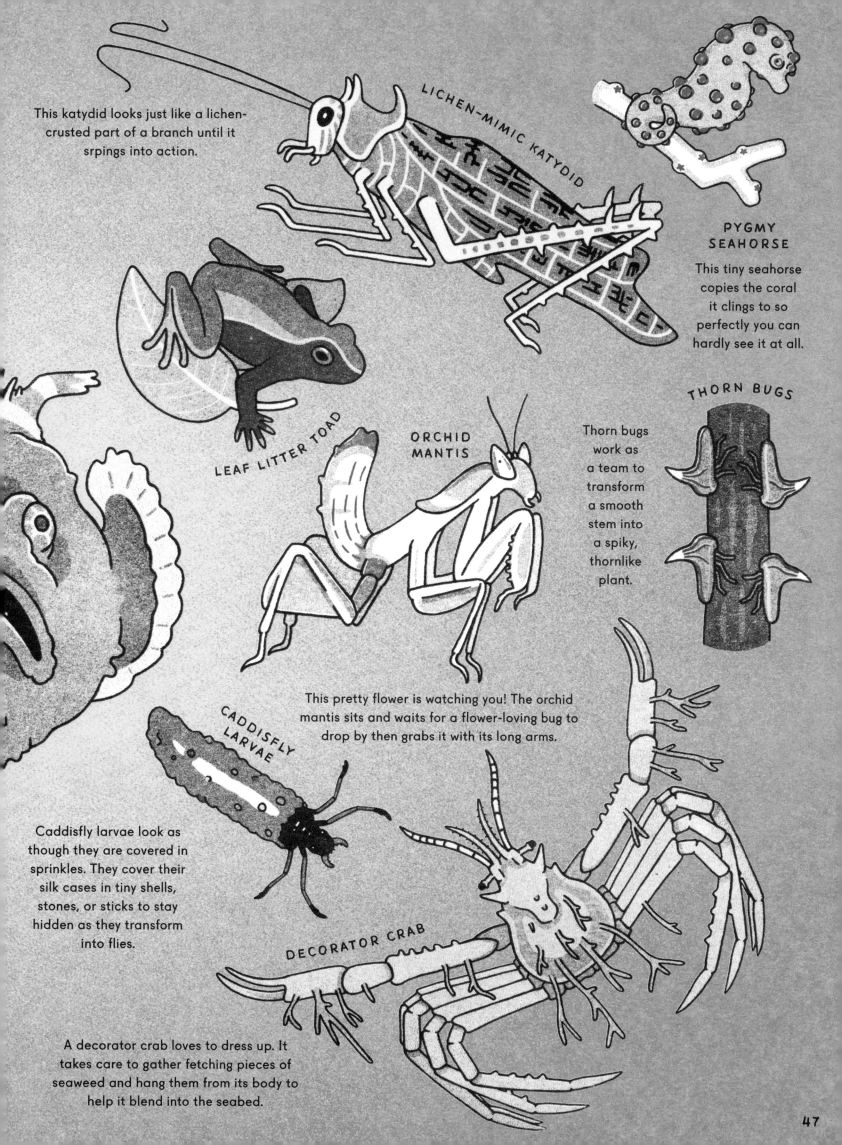

This katydid looks just like a lichen-crusted part of a branch until it srpings into action.

LICHEN-MIMIC KATYDID

PYGMY SEAHORSE

This tiny seahorse copies the coral it clings to so perfectly you can hardly see it at all.

LEAF LITTER TOAD

ORCHID MANTIS

THORN BUGS

Thorn bugs work as a team to transform a smooth stem into a spiky, thornlike plant.

This pretty flower is watching you! The orchid mantis sits and waits for a flower-loving bug to drop by then grabs it with its long arms.

CADDISFLY LARVAE

Caddisfly larvae look as though they are covered in sprinkles. They cover their silk cases in tiny shells, stones, or sticks to stay hidden as they transform into flies.

DECORATOR CRAB

A decorator crab loves to dress up. It takes care to gather fetching pieces of seaweed and hang them from its body to help it blend into the seabed.

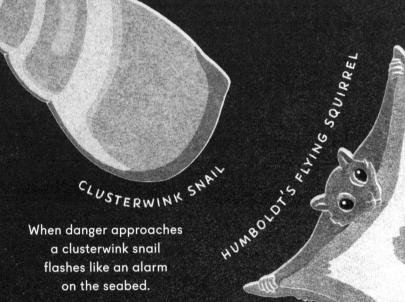

CLUSTERWINK SNAIL

When danger approaches a clusterwink snail flashes like an alarm on the seabed.

HUMBOLDT'S FLYING SQUIRREL

The fur of a Humboldt's flying squirrel glows hot pink under fluorescent light.

ANTARCTIC KRILL (GLOW-IN-THE-DARK)

CORAL (GLOW-IN-THE-DARK)

FIREFLY SQUID (BIOLUMINESCENT)

CRYSTAL JELLYFISH (BIOLUMINESCENT)

Flashlight fish flicker like fairy lights in the dark. They can blink their lights, which are underneath their eyes, on and off by closing a lid over them.

FLASHLIGHT FISH

LIGHT UP

In night skies, dark seas, and gloomy caves, creatures create a dazzling disco of colorful lights. Some animals make their own bright beams to flash a warning or to tempt their prey. Others secretly glow in a way that only they can see, but shine a fluorescent light and we can enter their neon world.

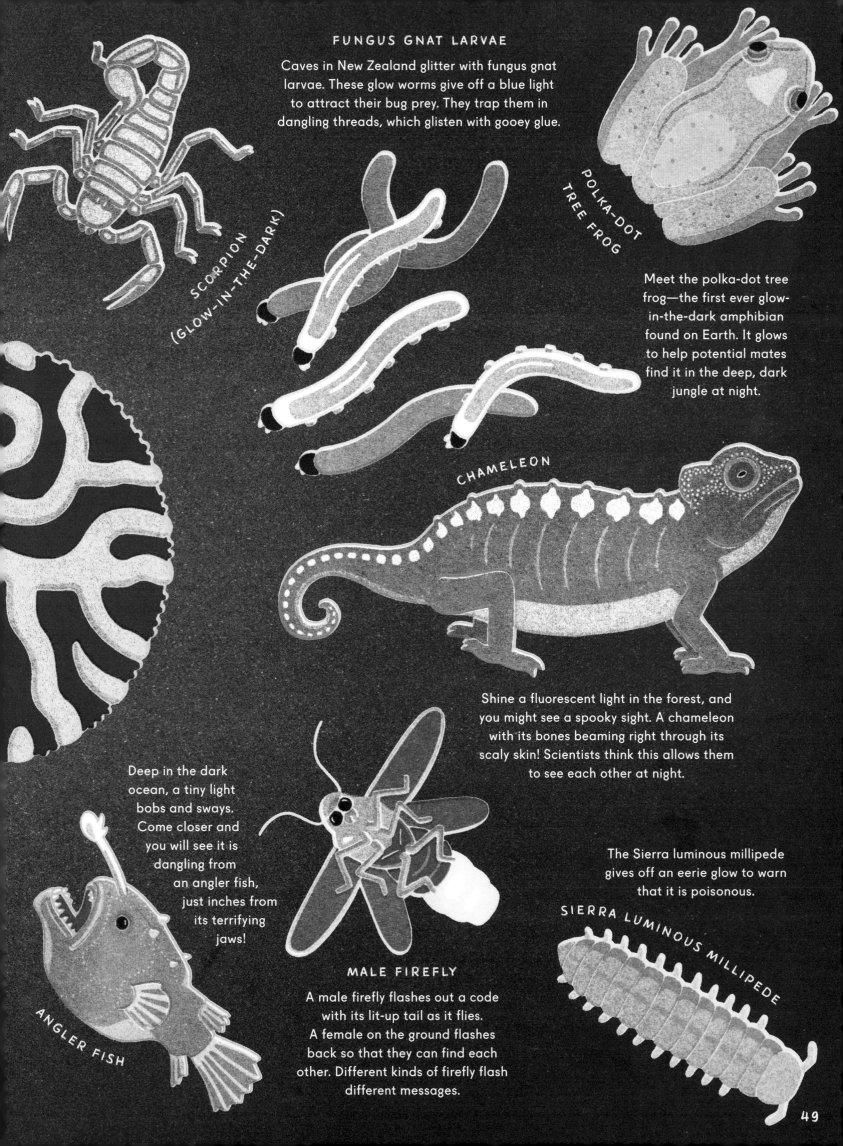

FUNGUS GNAT LARVAE

Caves in New Zealand glitter with fungus gnat larvae. These glow worms give off a blue light to attract their bug prey. They trap them in dangling threads, which glisten with gooey glue.

SCORPION (GLOW-IN-THE-DARK)

POLKA-DOT TREE FROG

Meet the polka-dot tree frog—the first ever glow-in-the-dark amphibian found on Earth. It glows to help potential mates find it in the deep, dark jungle at night.

CHAMELEON

Shine a fluorescent light in the forest, and you might see a spooky sight. A chameleon with its bones beaming right through its scaly skin! Scientists think this allows them to see each other at night.

Deep in the dark ocean, a tiny light bobs and sways. Come closer and you will see it is dangling from an angler fish, just inches from its terrifying jaws!

ANGLER FISH

The Sierra luminous millipede gives off an eerie glow to warn that it is poisonous.

SIERRA LUMINOUS MILLIPEDE

MALE FIREFLY

A male firefly flashes out a code with its lit-up tail as it flies. A female on the ground flashes back so that they can find each other. Different kinds of firefly flash different messages.

49

REGAL RING-NECKED SNAKE

A harmless regal ring-necked snake reveals its alarming, fiery underside to scare others away.

OCTOPUS

Who turned out the lights? An octopus can squirt a dark cloud of black ink to hide its getaway!

GARDEN TIGER MOTH

A garden tiger moth opens its camouflaged wings to reveal a burst of bright orange. It flutters to safety, leaving predators confused.

HAWK-HEADED PARROT

When the hawk-headed parrot gets ruffled it raises it red feathers to make itself look frightening.

FLAMBOYANT CUTTLEFISH

The flamboyant cuttlefish sends bands of color rippling down its body, putting its shrimp prey in a trance. Then the cuttlefish delivers a killer blow.

MEDITERRANEAN MANTIS

This mesmerizing mantis display puts off would-be predators.

THE 88 BUTTERFLY

Are you seeing double? The 88 butterfly has eye-boggling wings to confuse birds who might want to eat it.

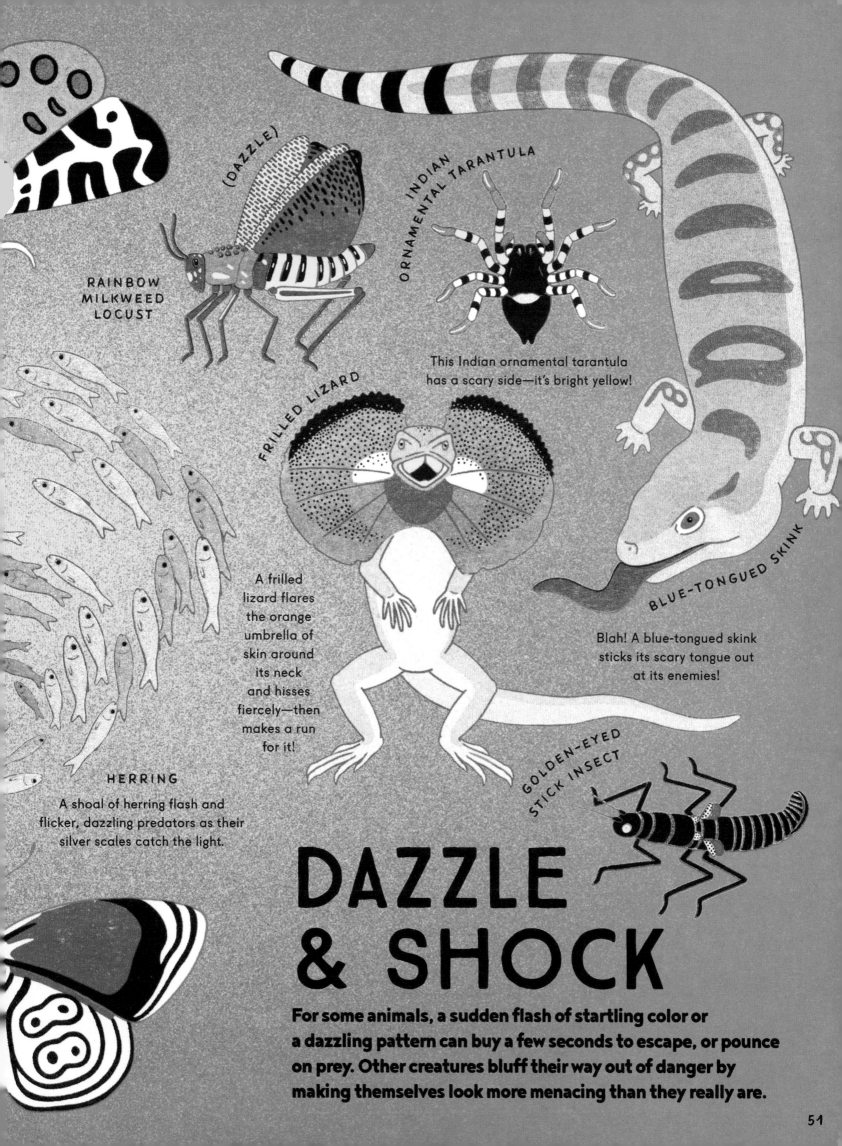

RAINBOW MILKWEED LOCUST

(DAZZLE)

INDIAN ORNAMENTAL TARANTULA

This Indian ornamental tarantula has a scary side—it's bright yellow!

FRILLED LIZARD

BLUE-TONGUED SKINK

A frilled lizard flares the orange umbrella of skin around its neck and hisses fiercely—then makes a run for it!

Blah! A blue-tongued skink sticks its scary tongue out at its enemies!

HERRING

A shoal of herring flash and flicker, dazzling predators as their silver scales catch the light.

GOLDEN-EYED STICK INSECT

DAZZLE & SHOCK

For some animals, a sudden flash of startling color or a dazzling pattern can buy a few seconds to escape, or pounce on prey. Other creatures bluff their way out of danger by making themselves look more menacing than they really are.

A hair-raising roar echoes through the jungle. It's a male Sumatran orangutan. His chubby cheek pads and long hair make him attractive to females but menacing to other males.

SUMATRAN ORANGUTAN

(MALE)

(FEMALE)

MANDARIN DUCKS

QUEEN ALEXANDRA'S BIRDWING BUTTERFLY

(MALE)

(FEMALE)

A male elephant seal weighs as much as a truck! He lumbers up to a much smaller female, inflates his trunk-like snout, and snorts loudly to let other males know she is his.

ELEPHANT SEAL

NORTHERN WHITE-CHEEKED GIBBON

Male red deer have large horns to fight off challengers and look menacing. Females are smaller and paler.

RED DEER

The male giraffe weevil uses his super-long neck as a weapon for battling other males.

GIRAFFE WEEVIL

ECLECTUS PARROT

For 100 years scientists thought the green male and red female eclectus parrot were different kinds of bird.

BLANKET OCTOPUS

A female blanket octopus flaps her fleshy cape to frighten off predators. She is 100 times larger than the teeny, ¾-in-long male.

(FEMALE)

(MALE)

NARWHAL

The narwhal is the unicorn of the sea, but only the male has a spiral tusk for fighting rivals.

MALES & FEMALES

Male and female animals often do different jobs, so their bodies don't always match! Sometimes they are a completely different size or shape. Often males are much more brightly colored to catch the ladies' eye!

GOLDEN ORB-WEAVER

Many female spiders are bigger and scarier than the male, just look at this golden orb weaver. She is ten times his size and is known to gobble up males without warning!

A big mane makes the male lion look threatening, but the faster female is the best hunter.

HERCULES BEETLE

LION

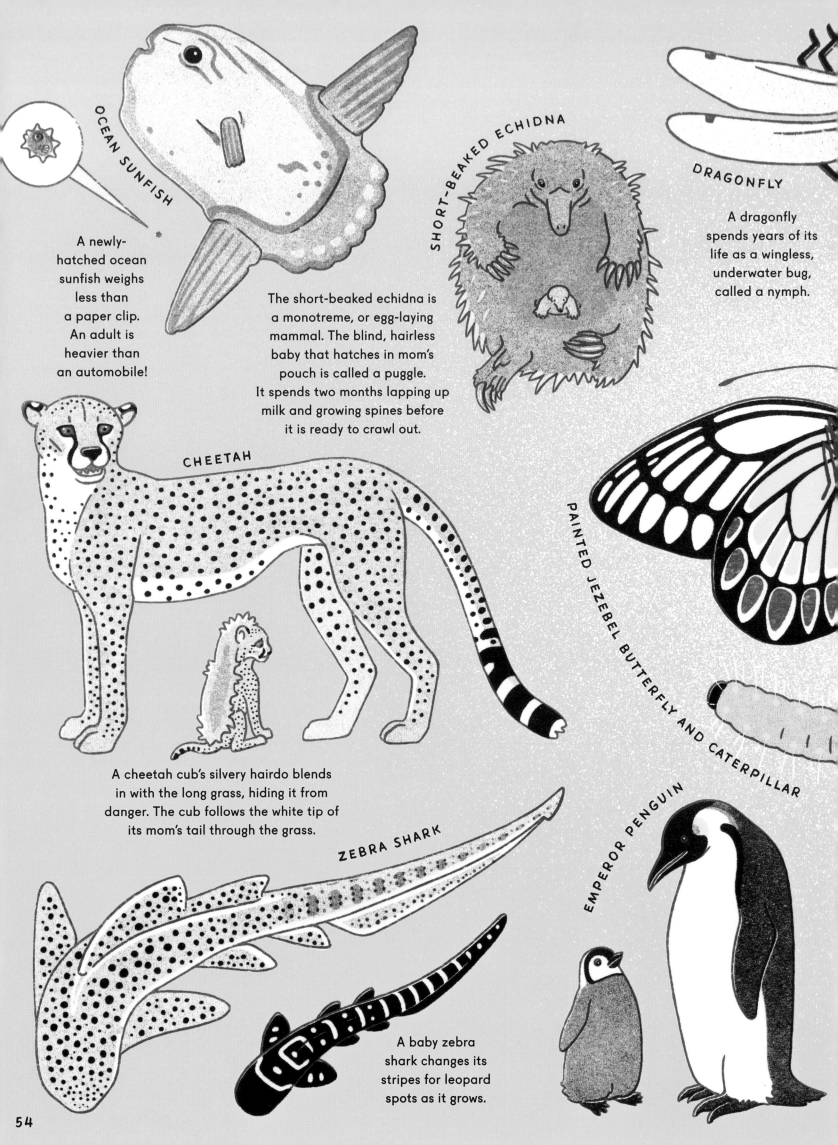

OCEAN SUNFISH

A newly-hatched ocean sunfish weighs less than a paper clip. An adult is heavier than an automobile!

SHORT-BEAKED ECHIDNA

The short-beaked echidna is a monotreme, or egg-laying mammal. The blind, hairless baby that hatches in mom's pouch is called a puggle. It spends two months lapping up milk and growing spines before it is ready to crawl out.

DRAGONFLY

A dragonfly spends years of its life as a wingless, underwater bug, called a nymph.

PAINTED JEZEBEL BUTTERFLY AND CATERPILLAR

CHEETAH

A cheetah cub's silvery hairdo blends in with the long grass, hiding it from danger. The cub follows the white tip of its mom's tail through the grass.

ZEBRA SHARK

A baby zebra shark changes its stripes for leopard spots as it grows.

EMPEROR PENGUIN

BABIES TO GROWN-UPS

Many baby animals look nothing like their parents. They might be camouflaged to protect them from predators or brightly colored so they don't get lost. Some tiny babies turn into giant grown-ups and others start life as different creatures altogether!

A silvery lutung baby is born with bright orange fur. This jungle-style hi-vis helps mom keep track of her little monkey.

SILVERY LUTUNG

CAMEL

A camel's fatty humps provide it with energy when food is hard to find. A baby camel does not need humps—it slurps its mother's milk.

A brown, stripy cassowary chick is hard to spot on the leafy forest floor. This camouflage keeps it safe from hungry passersby.

CASSOWARY

ZIMMERMAN'S POISON FROG

MATSCHIE'S TREE-KANGAROO

This Kangaroo's baby is called a joey and its born with nearly no hair. It waits in mom's pouch until it grows warm fur of its own.

This tiny tadpole rides on its parent's back until it's bigger.

55

HANUMAN LANGURS

In New Delhi, India, Hanuman langurs are trained to scare off other monkeys, causing mischief in return for food.

ROSE-RINGED PARAKEETS

Noisy flocks of rose-ringed parakeets live in parks across London, England. It is thought that they first appeared over fifty years ago, after a pair of pet parrots escaped their owners. Now you can spot their bright green wings against the gray London sky.

GRAY WOLVES

SIKA DEER

Usually sika deer lay low, staying hidden thanks to their dappled coats. But near Nara in Japan, they leave the safety of the forest and head for a sacred temple in the city, where they are fed by tourists.

Bangkok in Thailand was built on an area of wetland inhabited by reticulated pythons. In the wild, their markings help them camouflage against the scrub but now they are discovering drainpipes in the city provide even better cover!

RETICULATED PYTHONS

BRAZILIAN RUBY HUMMINGBIRD

SEA LION

WILD BOAR

Wild boar roam free in Berlin, Germany, rummaging for food. They mostly come out at night and root around under cover of darkness.

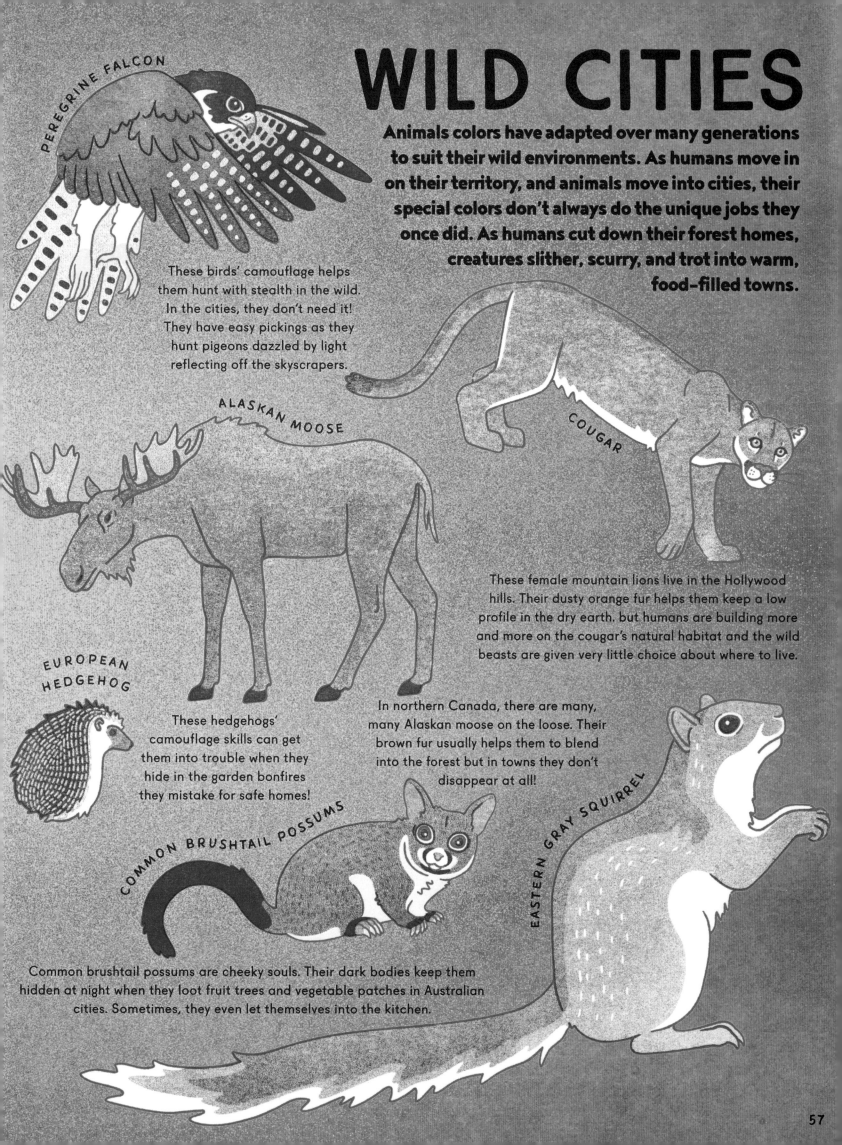

WILD CITIES

Animals colors have adapted over many generations to suit their wild environments. As humans move in on their territory, and animals move into cities, their special colors don't always do the unique jobs they once did. As humans cut down their forest homes, creatures slither, scurry, and trot into warm, food-filled towns.

PEREGRINE FALCON

These birds' camouflage helps them hunt with stealth in the wild. In the cities, they don't need it! They have easy pickings as they hunt pigeons dazzled by light reflecting off the skyscrapers.

ALASKAN MOOSE

COUGAR

These female mountain lions live in the Hollywood hills. Their dusty orange fur helps them keep a low profile in the dry earth. but humans are building more and more on the cougar's natural habitat and the wild beasts are given very little choice about where to live.

EUROPEAN HEDGEHOG

These hedgehogs' camouflage skills can get them into trouble when they hide in the garden bonfires they mistake for safe homes!

In northern Canada, there are many, many Alaskan moose on the loose. Their brown fur usually helps them to blend into the forest but in towns they don't disappear at all!

EASTERN GRAY SQUIRREL

COMMON BRUSHTAIL POSSUMS

Common brushtail possums are cheeky souls. Their dark bodies keep them hidden at night when they loot fruit trees and vegetable patches in Australian cities. Sometimes, they even let themselves into the kitchen.

CARING FOR CREATURES

BEE FRIENDLY!

Bees and butterflies feed on flower nectar. Grow some of their favorite flowers in your garden or a pot. Place a dish of water and pebbles nearby for them to perch on and drink.

Make a shady shelter for creepy-crawlies in a corner of your garden, balcony, or windowsill. Just fill an old flower pot with twigs, pine cones, and dead leaves and see who comes to stay.

BIRD CAFE

GO GREEN

Serve up sunflower seeds and oats for feathered friends to eat. Hang up bottles and tubs to make birdy snack stations.

Talk to grown-ups about buying planet-friendly cleaning products. Chemicals that get washed down drains end up in rivers and oceans, harming the animals that live there.

Our planet is a colorful wonderland. All you need need to do to discover it is to step outside! Go on a mini safari and stumble upon the birds and bugs in your garden, and wild animals in your neighborhood. Find out what you can do to shelter them, feed them, and keep them safe.

LOOK AND LEAVE

Stick to paths when you go for a walk. Don't pick flowers, nuts, or leaves, or trample or break plants as these provide homes or food for bugs and wild animals.

HOME SWEET HOME

If you find any nests, dens, or burrows, don't disturb them, even if they seem empty. You might frighten away the wild homeowners.

TAKE CARE

If you spot any wild creatures in parks, woods, or ponds, watch from a distance. Getting too close could scare the animals or put you in danger.

WHAT GARBAGE?

Plastic bottles, cans, and wrappers can harm wildlife, and so can scraps of human food. Make sure you take your trash home and recycle it if you can.

GLOSSARY

Animal experts use these special words when describing animals, their behavior, life cycles, and lifestyles. On this page, find out what they mean and then you will be able to start talking like an animal expert, too.

ALBINO
A person or animal born with a medical condition that results in very pale skin, white hair, and pink eyes.

ALGAE
Simple plants that have no leaves or stems and grow in or near water.

AMPHIBIAN
An animal that can live on land and in water.

ANTENNAE
Thin feelers on the head of an animal that are used to touch things.

ARCTIC
The very cold sea and land in the north of the world.

BLOOD VESSEL
A thin tube that carries blood around a person's or animal's body.

BOWER
A shady place under the branches of a tree.

BURROW
A hole in the ground that an animal lives in.

CAMOUFLAGED
When something looks like its surroundings.

CHIRRUPING
Making a short high-pitched sound.

CHRYSALIS
The hard case that covers a moth or butterfly before it turns into an adult with wings.

COMB
A soft growth on a chicken's head.

CORAL
A rocklike material made in the sea from the bodies of tiny creatures.

CYANIDE
A powerful poison that can kill.

DAZZLE
When a pattern is so bright or busy that it confuses the animal looking at it.

FANG
A long, sharp tooth.

FIN
A thin, flat part that stands out from a fish's body and helps it to swim.

FLUORESCENT
Very bright colors that can be seen in the dark.

FRONDS
Large, divided leaves, like those of palm trees and ferns.

GILL
The part on either side of a fish through which it breathes.

HATCH
To break out of an egg.

IRIDESCENT
Showing bright colors that change with movement.

KALEIDOSCOPE
A changing mixture or pattern.

LARVAE
The stage of an bug or animal when it has left its egg but has not yet grown into an adult bug or animal.

LURE
To attract a person or animal.

MAMMAL
An animal that has hair and the female can feed its babies with its own milk.

MONOCHROME
The colors black, white, and gray, or just one color.

MONOTREME
Mammals that lay eggs—the platypus and echidnas.

MORPH
To change from one thing to another.

MUCUS
A sticky, wet liquid produced by the body.

NEON
An extremely bright, almost glowing, color.

PIGMENT
The natural substance that gives animals and plants their color.

PLAIN
A large area of flat land without trees.

PREDATOR
An animal that lives by killing and eating other animals.

PREEN
When a bird uses its beak to clean its feathers.

PREY
Any animal that is hunted and killed by another animal for food.

PSYCHEDELIC
Having bright colors and strange patterns.

REEF
A line of rocks just below or just above the surface of the sea.

SCALES
Small, thin pieces of hard skin or bone that cover the outside of animals such as fish and snakes.

SCALY
Covered with scales.

SHOAL/SCHOOL
A large number of fish swimming as a group.

SNOUT
An animal's nose and mouth sticking out from the rest of its face.

TENTACLE
One of the long, thin parts of a sea animal that are used for feeling, holding, and moving.

TERRITORY
An area that an animal or group of animals uses and fights to keep.

TOXIC
Poisonous.

TRANCE
A state that is like being asleep, not in control of the body.

VENOM
A poison produced by an animal, such as a snake or bug, and used to kill another animal by biting or stinging.

VERTEBRATE
An animal that has a backbone.

VIPER
A type of poisonous snake.

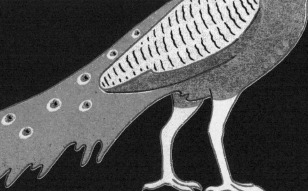

INDEX

Brimming with creative inspiration, how-to projects, and useful information to enrich your everyday life, Quarto Knows is a favorite destination for those pursuing their interests and passions. Visit our site and dig deeper with our books into your area of interest: Quarto Creates, Quarto Cooks, Quarto Homes, Quarto Lives, Quarto Drives, Quarto Explores, Quarto Gifts, or Quarto Kids.

The illustrations were created using risography
Set in Palomino Sans, True North and Fugue

Published by Georgia Amson-Bradshaw
Designed by Karissa Santos and Sasha Moxon
Commissioned and edited by Lucy Brownridge
Production by Dawn Cameron

Manufactured in Guangdong, China CC112020

9 8 7 6 5 4 3 2 1